# HELP YOUR CHILD LEARN TO READ

## Betty Root M.B.E.

Tutor in Charge, Reading and Language
Information Centre, University of Reading

### Edited by Robyn Gee

### Designed by Mary Cartwright

**Illustrated by Brenda Haw and Teri Gower**
**Photographs by Bob Mazzer and John Bellenis**
**Airbrush work by David Gillingwater**

# Contents

# ABOUT THIS BOOK

Parents have a very important role to play in helping their children learn to read. Until recently many people believed that teaching reading should be left entirely to teachers. All the recent studies on this subject show, however, that the right kind of help and support from their parents is of enormous benefit to children.

Learning to read involves bringing together a lot of different skills, that a child can start acquiring very early on in life. The first section of the book will help you to understand what these skills are and give you some ideas on how to help your child develop them as a general preparation for learning to read.

You will then find some useful guidelines for when your child is ready to start looking at words and letters more carefully. At this stage you may well find that playing some simple games is the best way to help your child start to recognize and read her first words and sentences. General advice on playing games is followed by some ideas for word games to make and play.

Once your child can recognize several words she may like to start reading aloud with you.

This may sound like a big step to take, but pages 20 to 23 will help you to decide whether your child is ready and tell you exactly how to go about it. When she recognizes quite a number of words, you could start playing some letter and sound games together.

At some stage of your child's reading progress the influence of school and teacher will become important. Pages 40 to 45 will help you to understand what goes on in school and how to work with it to help your child.

This is followed by advice on what to do if you suspect your child has problems with reading.

Always remember that the most important thing you can do is to help your child enjoy books. Allow her to progress at her own pace; always encourage but don't try to force her to go too quickly.

# TALKING

Talking and reading are closely connected. Encourage children to express themselves in words by providing plenty of interesting things for them to talk about.

There is a strong link between language development and learning to read. It is clear that before being able to read children must know and use a good basic vocabulary. They can only understand words they see in print if they have already come across them in speech.

Research has shown that children who are good talkers tend to become good readers. The best way of encouraging children's language development is to take time to talk to them. Encourage them to express opinions, ask questions and take decisions. Don't restrict your own language too much in your conversations, but discuss and explain new words whenever your child shows an interest. Children learn new words by hearing them used in context. You can talk about the sound of the words, other words with similar sounds or meanings and words that mean the opposite.

Children also learn a great deal by listening to the conversations going on around them. This is one

## Fantasy play

Play in which children imagine themselves in other roles or situations encourages them to try out new words, phrases and ways of expressing themselves.

**Puppets.** Specialists often use these with children who have speech and other communication problems. They can be made very quickly in a variety of different ways. Some children just play with puppets in the same way as they do with dolls. Some may want to put on a show. Some children really dislike puppets so don't push them if they are not interested.

**Boxes.** Cardboard boxes of all shapes and sizes are very useful for creating a great variety of different play situations. Extra-large ones make wonderful houses, castles, caves and dens. Medium ones can be made into vehicles, tables, desks and counters, while smaller ones make miniature garages, farms, and houses.

**Dressing up.** Try to build up a selection of dressing-up clothes and accessories by collecting friends' and relations' throw-outs and looking at rummage sales and in second-hand shops. Children often regard dressing-up accessories, such as hats, jewellery and bags, as more important than clothes.

reason for providing children with the company both of other children and adults, especially if your family is small in number.

It is important not to discourage children from talking by correcting what they say or criticizing the way they express themselves, or by trying to stop them using baby language. You can demonstrate the correct way of saying something by bringing it into your own conversations.

Providing interesting and stimulating activities is an important part of encouraging language development. Children must have something they want to express before they can use and practise new words, phrases and expressions that they have acquired. Going on outings, playing with toys, playing games and making things all provide experiences to talk about. Below are a few ideas which are particularly good for encouraging children to express themselves in words.

## Television and language development

There is no doubt that television can help to enrich a child's vocabulary. In order to make the best use of television, try to watch with your child and discuss together what you have seen. If a child watches alone a great deal it is easy for him to get in the habit of giving only half his attention when watching or listening to something.

## Descriptive games

Games which require children to describe things encourage them to search for the words they need and help them to speak and think more clearly.

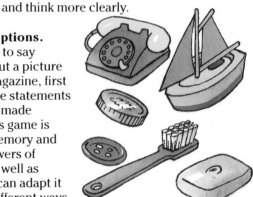

**Picture descriptions.** Take it in turns to say something about a picture in a book or magazine, first repeating all the statements that have been made previously. This game is good for the memory and developing powers of observation as well as language. You can adapt it in numerous different ways e.g "On my magic island I would have ...."

**Feely box.** Put household objects in a box with hand-holes cut in the side. Your child then puts his hands in the box and tries to describe what he can feel before guessing what it is.

A more advanced version can be played with three people. One person puts an object in the box, the second feels and tries to describe it, the third guesses what it is.

**Connections.** Simple games which require children to describe the connection between two objects, or a set of objects, certainly help to develop language. Use real objects from around the house or garden, or draw simple pictures on small pieces of card. Get children to collect their own pairs of objects too, and explain why they go together.

# LISTENING

Listening is a skill which has to be learned through practice.

Being able to listen properly plays a very important part in learning and communication in general and is essential in the first stages of learning to read. Children begin to read words mainly by the look of them, but soon realize that they are made up of individual and groups of sounds.

Children have to learn to listen through practice. Life today is much noisier than it used to be and many children are accustomed to quite a high level of background noise. This can mean that they get used to shutting out sound and only half-listening.

They need encouragement to listen with attention. There are a number of things you can do to help them such as pointing out different sounds and talking about them and playing games to encourage listening.

## Listening games

**How many sounds?** Get children to close their eyes and keep very still and quiet, then see how many sounds they can hear. You can play this inside or out.

**What am I doing now?** One person closes their eyes and has to guess what the other is doing – things like opening a door, bouncing a ball, turning the pages of a newspaper.

**Whispered instructions.** Start with just one instruction such as "sit on a cushion", then add more one at a time … "find a book", "give teddy a hug".

**Tape recorded sounds.** Go round the house with your child and record a variety of sounds, such as a tap running, a clock ticking, vacuuming, keys turning in a lock. Can he recognize them easily when you play the tape back?

You could draw pictures to represent the sounds on pieces of card. As he hears each sound the child has to turn over the card which matches it.

**Shake and match.** You need a good selection of empty containers with lids. (Film canisters, or cottage cheese cartons both work well.) Put a small amount of different substances, such as sand, pebbles, rice, paper-clips, or sugar into them. Put the same substance into two of the containers. Your child has to shake the containers and match the ones that are the same.

You can then shake three containers, one after the other. Your child has to remember the order in which the sounds were made, find the right sounds and repeat exactly.

# RHYME AND RHYTHM

Experts are only just beginning to realize the importance of rhyme in learning to read. It is now known from extensive research that children who find it hard to recognize which words rhyme with each other often have difficulty in learning to read. This sheds new light on the importance of sharing nursery rhymes, action rhymes and simple poems with small children. Besides buying a good book of nursery rhymes, it is also worth considering some of the excellent tapes and records that are available.

The rhythm of poems and songs helps children to remember the words. When they know a song or poem by heart show them the words in print. This helps them to understand the way in which the written word represents the sung or spoken word.

Appreciation of rhyme helps with learning to read.

## Games with rhyme and rhythm

Most children enjoy playing around with rhyme once they have got the idea. Some children find it very difficult. If you get a blank response when you try to introduce your child to rhyming games, just leave it for a while and try again after a few weeks.

### Odd one out

like, bike, water, spike.

Say a list of words, all but one of which rhyme. See if your child can spot the odd one.

### Rhyming clues

I am thinking of a word that rhymes with "cook". You read it.

You give the rhyming clues and your child has to guess what word you are thinking of.

I Spy with my little eye something that rhymes with "hat". It says "meow".

You can turn rhyming clues into a rhyming version of "I Spy" if you like.

**Rhyming box.** Put a selection of objects in a box. Take turns to take one out and see how many words you can each think of which rhyme with it.

**Tap out a rhythm.** See if your child can copy simple rhythms tapped out with a spoon or pencil. You could also use the shakers described opposite.

# SHARING BOOKS

Sharing books with adults helps children to become readers.

It is important that children see their parents reading for pleasure.

Books form a bond between the people who enjoy them together.

The most important thing that parents can do to encourage their children to become readers is to look at, read and enjoy books together. If children see books as a source of pleasure, entertainment and information, they have a strong incentive to learn to read.

When a child looks at books with an adult, her pleasure comes not just from looking at pictures and listening to stories. The individual attention you give her, the physical closeness, the feeling of warmth and security will all contribute to her feelings about books. Conversely, be careful never to force books on a child who would clearly prefer to be doing something else.

## Parents' attitude to books

A child's attitude to books is also going to be conditioned by what she perceives her parents' attitude to be. If she sees her parents enjoying reading books themselves and referring to books for information, she is much more likely to think of books as enjoyable and useful.

## Learning about books and words

A child who is used to using books will already have absorbed a lot of information that is needed before learning to read. She will understand, for instance, that you always start at the front and work towards the back and that you tackle each page from top to bottom and from left to right; that pictures can help you to understand the words; that words are separated by blank spaces; that stories have a beginning, a middle and an end and often follow a predictable pattern.

## Other benefits

Sharing books with a child is also an excellent way of helping to develop her powers of understanding and speech, listening and concentration, and observation, all of which are themselves important in the process of learning to read.

There are many other good reasons for sharing books with children besides helping them on their way to reading. Books form a bond between the people who enjoy them together. They stimulate the imagination and encourage emotional development as the child begins to appreciate how other people feel. They extend her knowledge of the world by introducing her to new situations and deepening her understanding of those she has already experienced.

## When to start?

It is never too early to introduce a child to books. Tiny babies can enjoy the movement of the pages turning, the noise of the paper and the sound of your voice, as you talk or read. To begin with, they see the pictures simply as colours, shapes and patterns. Gradually the shapes become familiar and recognizable and they start to associate specific sounds with each shape. Then they learn to turn the pages by themselves, to point to things they recognize, to name things. Soon they will be talking about the pictures they see and then following a sequence of pictures through a book and listening to the words that go with them

## How often?

Use books with your child as often as she wants to and you can find the time. With babies, and especially with toddlers, you will probably find that very brief spells of looking at books at frequent intervals throughout the day work best. As your child's concentration span extends you will find your book sessions lengthening and becoming less frequent. You can gradually introduce special times of day for looking at books together. Try at the very least always to have one book sharing session each day. If you choose a special time – before a nap or bedtime – it will quickly become a habit. Remember, though, if your child is too tired, or just not in the mood for books, don't insist.

## Looking at books alone

Shared pleasure is an important ingredient of early experiences with books, but it is also worth getting across from an early age that books can be enjoyable when looked at by yourself. Encourage a baby from the beginning to look at books on her own.

She will start by simply playing with them, but later on she may be happy to spend short periods looking at the pictures by herself. This is more likely to happen if she is used to seeing people around her looking at books.

## A place to keep books

It is worth taking some trouble to find a special place for children to keep their books. Some people keep a few in several different rooms so that there is always a selection close at hand. Low shelves that children can reach easily, or specially decorated boxes close to somewhere comfortable to sit will encourage children into the habit of looking at books by themselves.

Try not to be too protective of books, but teach children not to tear them or write in them. You can cover special favourites with self-adhesive plastic to give them a longer life.

# Choice of early books

To start with, choose a few books that have clear, simple, colourful pictures of things that are part of a baby's everyday world. There should be only one or two per page and no confusing detail.

From as early as three months the baby will be able to focus briefly on the pictures. From about 12 months, as she acquires more words, she will gradually be able to cope with more complicated pictures.

Invest in a good nursery rhyme book at an early stage. It will remind you of old favourites and perhaps introduce you to some new ones. Nursery rhymes usually remain popular for a long time, so choose a good sturdy edition with interesting illustrations.

Pop-ups, books with flaps to lift and tags to pull, "feely" books, squeaky books, board and bath books are good for getting babies and toddlers involved with books. They need to be tough to last.

You may be able to start introducing some very simple story books from about 18 months onwards. Choose stories with few words and plenty of pictures which do a lot of the storytelling work.

The words will only gradually become as important as the pictures. Stories which repeat catchy, rhythmical phrases over and over again give toddlers something to listen for and enjoy even when they cannot really follow the storyline.

Stories involving familiar everyday routines are also popular with toddlers. They like to explore how like or unlike other people they are. They may also enjoy fantasy stories but it is worth watching out for, and taking seriously, any sign of a child being disturbed or frightened by a story.

It is useful for a child to realize that books are a source of factual information as well as stories. Once she starts to outgrow her first simple picture books, replace them with some information books. Zoos, farms and vehicles are popular subjects.

Books are also useful for learning about things like colours, shapes, sizes, numbers and letters.

As your child gets older, introduce her to as great a variety as possible: books with different types of illustration, some detailed, some simple; books with different subject matter; books of different size, shape and length. Be guided by your own taste, but follow your child's enthusiasms. Make use of libraries so that you can experiment at no expense.

# "Reading" the pictures

Children who have plenty of opportunity to look at pictures in books and talk about them learn to read pictures to find out what is going on in them. This is very useful when they first start to read, as clues from the pictures give them confidence to try the words underneath.

Books without words, where the pictures tell the entire story are useful for encouraging this skill. You can carry this a stage further by trying some simple picture-sequencing activities.

Draw a simple picture sequence or cut one out from a comic. Three pictures are enough to start with.

Get your child to talk about each picture and then to put them in order from left to right telling the story at the same time.

Putting things in order from left to right is an important part of learning to read. If things are not in the right order they do not make sense.

## Books and television

Use television to help stimulate a child's interest in books. Follow up programmes she has enjoyed by finding books on the same subject. Children who otherwise show little interest in books may start to enjoy them by looking at books based on their favourite programmes. Don't let television become a substitute for books and don't allow television to compete with books for a child's attention.

## Story tapes

Story tapes are excellent for all sorts of occasions when you cannot give your child your full attention but they are no substitute for the adult interest and company that reading to a child provides. Children will want some books read to them over and over and over again. You may find it helpful to record the story for them so that they can hear it whenever they want. A familiar voice reading will probably be appreciated more by a small child than a bought tape. Don't forget to record some signal to indicate when they should turn each page.

11

# DRAWING ATTENTION TO WORDS

Long before children are ready to start learning to read you can help them to develop a general awareness of the written word and of its usefulness in all sorts of everyday situations. Point out words on signs and labels and make your child aware of all the different situations in which you use reading and writing to gain and impart information.

## Labels and captions

Writing things down for children is a good way of getting them interested in written words. Seeing their own name written down interests most small children and the first letter of their own name is usually the first letter they recognize.

Write labels they can put on their possessions or in special places.

Write captions for pictures they have drawn or painted. Get them to tell you exactly what to write.

## Books

Make children aware that the printed words on the page are telling you what to say when you read them a story. If your child seems interested you could single out a word that frequently recurs and show it to her, telling her what it says.

You could also bring this point home by making your own book together. Tie or staple together some folded sheets of paper, choose a subject, get your child to draw the pictures and tell you what to write underneath them.

Tie together with ribbon or string.

## Shopping

Cut out logos and pictures from old packets and wrappers and stick them onto pieces of card. When you go shopping your child can take the appropriate cards and help you find what you want by matching them to the goods on the shelves.

Get children to help you make shopping lists and ask them to cross out or tick off each item as you find it.

You could write the first letter of each word in a different colour.

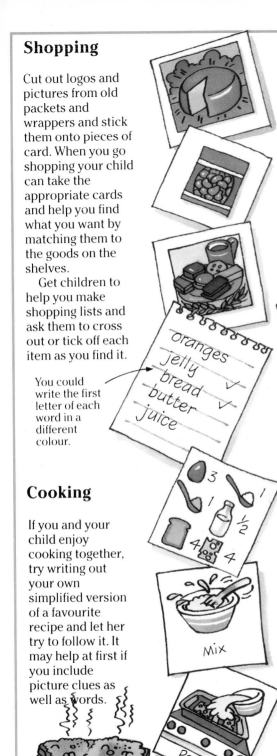

## Cooking

If you and your child enjoy cooking together, try writing out your own simplified version of a favourite recipe and let her try to follow it. It may help at first if you include picture clues as well as words.

## Signs and maps

Make a mental note of some of the signs you see on regular walks or shopping expeditions. Write them on pieces of card. When you go for walks see if children can match the card to the sign. After several successful times at this, see if they can recognize any of the words when they get home.

When a child can recognize quite a few signs make a very simple map of your local area. Use it together to decide which way you will go for walks. Encourage your child to match the words she sees on the route to the words on the map.

On longer journeys write a list of places you will pass through and other signs you may see. See how many of them you can spot together.

## Television

Use a newspaper with your child to help you decide which programmes she can watch. You could write out the names of the programmes on separate pieces of card and draw on a clock showing the appropriate starting time. Let her decide when to switch on by matching the clock to a real clock or watch.

# STARTING TO RECOGNIZE WORDS AND LETTERS

As children get used to looking at books, seeing things written down and noticing words in their environment, they will gradually be able to recognize some words and individual letters. At this stage you may find yourself faced with several questions: Should you be concentrating on words or letters? What should you call the letters? How should you write them? Below are a few simple guidelines.

teapot

umbrella

Patrick

coat hook

## Recognizing words

When children first start to recognize letters and words it is better to concentrate on showing them words, especially those that have real meaning for them, such as the names of friends, family, pets and toys. When you show them a word, say it several times, but not too obtrusively.

Don't try to teach isolated words without giving some context or clue as to their meaning. Pictures with words, labels on objects, signs in situations all give words a context. Getting children to memorize isolated words written on "flashcards" does not. It is a big breakthrough when a child can recognize words on their own. Don't expect this too soon.

## Capital letters and small letters

Many capital letters are very different in shape to their small (lower case) equivalents. To make it easier concentrate at first on small letters.* They give words distinctive shapes, whereas capitals make words uniform in shape. However, use capitals where common sense suggests it, such as for the first letters of names.

monkey       MONKEY

Distinctive shape.    Uniform shape.

## Recognizing letters

There does come a time when unknown words present problems. They cannot always be recognized as whole words, or guessed in context. At this stage a child needs other ways of working out what a word says. Knowing the sound of the first letter can provide a powerful clue. Concentrate only on initial letter sounds, though. In the early stages of learning to read it is not a good idea to try to teach children to "sound out" each letter of a word (c-a-t). They find it hard to understand what they are being asked to do.

When you first teach letter sounds always use

Public Library

Post Office

Yes, there's another "p" for Peter.

Peter

## Letter sounds and letter names

You need to teach children the sound made by each letter, but they do not usually find it difficult to learn letter sounds and letter names almost at the same time.

This is the letter "b" and it says "buh".

words your child already knows. Most children start by recognizing the first letter of their own name and the names of people and things close to them. They then start spotting these when they appear in different contexts.

## The alphabet

There are many good alphabet books and friezes which help children to learn letter shapes and sounds. Don't be in a hurry to teach them alphabetical order, although you may be surprised at how quickly they learn it.

14

*See page 33 for the correct way to form the letters of the alphabet for a child.

# PLAYING GAMES

It is important to keep in mind that the best thing you can do to help your child learn to read, is to read to her and with her and have plenty of interesting books around. Making her aware of the written word in her surroundings and writing things down for her are also very helpful. If you want to do a little more than this you can play games to help with word and letter recognition.

Games can provide a relaxed and informal learning situation, free from tension and anxiety. Children are actively involved and are required to respond and make decisions. In playing a game children can see a limited number of words lots of times, but not in a boring or repetitive way.

Playing with words should be fun and should promote the idea that learning to read is enjoyable. Only play when your child wants to. Don't make it appear a duty or a chore or a specially important activity. These games should fit in alongside other play activities you share with your child.

Give lots of praise and encouragement and avoid giving her any idea of failure. If a game is too hard, help her with it, adapt it to suit her, or tactfully move on to another one.

Games can provide a relaxed and informal learning situation.

Magnetic letters

Alphabet bricks

## Making up games

On the following pages are some suggestions for games and activities you can make and play with your child. You may also like to make up some games of your own. At first your main objective should be to find entertaining ways of:

• Matching a word to a picture.

• Matching a written word to a spoken word.

• Matching a written word to a written word.

• Matching an initial letter and a picture.

• Matching letter shapes to letter sounds.

## Other activities

There are many good games and activities which you can buy to help with word and letter recognition. Magnetic letters which stick to refrigerators and washing machines are a particularly good purchase. They have the great advantage of being easy to move around, which is very helpful when children are beginning to build words. Children can feel the different letter shapes with their hands and this helps them to distinguish and remember each letter.

Alphabet puzzle

Picture word lotto ➔

# SOME WORD GAMES TO MAKE AND PLAY

## Materials

- Plenty of paper and card, such as lining paper, wallpaper (use the back), cereal and other packets, plain postcards and old greetings cards.
- Scissors
- Glue
- Ruler
- Coloured pens
- A good supply of pictures to cut out (Catalogues showing toys, clothes and household goods are ideal.)

## Points to bear in mind

- When making a game, select words which your child has already seen in other contexts and which are part of his vocabulary.
- It is worth taking care of the presentation of a game. If it is carefully made it will probably be more attractive to your child.
- Consider adapting any of these games to give it a theme that will particularly appeal to your child.
- You can also adapt any game to make it easier or harder, or more or less competitive according to the abilities and temperament of your child. Most of the games can be adapted to include more players.

## Make a line

### To make

- Cut out a baseboard approximately 10½ in square.
- Draw lines to divide it into nine squares as shown below.
- Cut out nine cards to fit the squares on the board.
- Stick a picture on one side of each card and, on the other, write the corresponding word and draw a circle the size of a counter.
- Find ten counters, five of one colour, five of another.

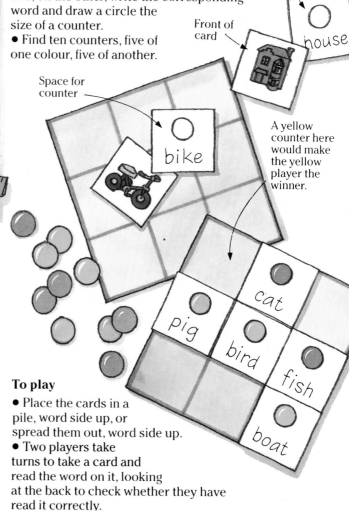

Back of card

Front of card

Space for counter

A yellow counter here would make the yellow player the winner.

### To play

- Place the cards in a pile, word side up, or spread them out, word side up.
- Two players take turns to take a card and read the word on it, looking at the back to check whether they have read it correctly.
- If a player reads a word correctly, he places the card on a space on the board and places a counter on it.
- Each player uses a different coloured counter and the aim of the game is to make a line of three counters all the same colour, along the lines of "Tic Tac Toe".
- Sometimes neither player can make a line. If this happens, shuffle the cards and start again.

# Stepping stones

**To make**
- Cut out a number of large cardboard or paper circles.
- On each circle write the name of one of the family or a friend.

**To play**
- Call out instructions such as "Jump on Mom".
- The child has to find the right card and keep jumping up and down until the next instruction is received.
- If you are playing with more than one child you could make a set of identical cards for each player.

Later you can turn this into a sentence building game. Include verbs and other parts of speech. Children have to jump on them in the right order to make a sentence.

# Odd word out

**To make**
- If you come across a large, interesting, busy picture in an old magazine or on a calendar or piece of wrapping paper, save it and cut it out.
- On smaller pieces of card write the names of some things that appear in the picture and some that do not.

**To play**

Children have to sort out which words belong to the picture and which do not.

You can later make the game harder by writing sentences instead of words.

If this activity succeeds you will probably find yourself making several different sets of pictures with words. It is worth marking each picture and its accompanying words with a particular logo or colour to stop different sets getting muddled.

Logo

17

## Choose your word

**To make**
- On a strip of card draw or stick a simple picture.
- Beside the picture write a choice of three words – one to match the picture and two which look similar to it.
- On the back of the card colour a space to indicate the correct word.
- Find a paper-clip.

**To play**
Children have to decide which word matches the picture and put the paper-clip on the space beside it. They can check their answer by turning the card over.

Front of card

| | spit | |
|---|---|---|
| | spider | |
| | spot | |

Back of card

spider

Colour the space behind the correct word.

| boot | |
|---|---|
| bath | |
| boat | |

| Polly likes to play | football | |
|---|---|---|
| | bed | |
| | kitchen | |

You can vary this game by writing simple sentences and giving a choice of words to end them.

## Story words

**To make**
- Find a fairly short story which your child knows quite well.
- Pick out some of the key words and write each one on a small piece of card. At first it is easiest to choose nouns.

**To play with one child**
- Read the words on the cards with your child.
- Read the story, stopping when you come to a word you know is on one of the cards.
- The child has to guess what the word might be and then look to see if she can find it on her cards.

**To play with more than one child**
- Read the words on the cards with the children.
- Shuffle the cards and deal them out equally between the children.
- Start reading the story fairly slowly.
- Children bang the table or signal in some way when you read one of the words they have in front of them.

medium sized bowl for Mother bear and a tiny little bowl for baby bear.

The porridge was rather hot so the three bears went for a walk in the wood while it

bowl

spoon

chair

porridge

bed

- If they signal correctly they turn over the appropriate card and you continue reading. (In most stories the key words occur quite frequently, so if a child misses a word there is usually another chance to hear it.)
- The first player to turn over all her cards is the winner.

## True or false

**To make**
- Cut out two baseboards and mark them up as shown.
- Cut 12 pieces of card to fit the squares on the board.
- Make up 12 simple sentences about your family and friends. Six of them should be true and six false.
- Write the sentences on the cards.

Cards

A pig can fly

Daddy has grey hair

Alfie has three legs

Baseboards

T T T F F F
T T T F F F

**To play**
- One player has the "True" board, the other has the "False" board.
- Shuffle the cards and place them face down between the players.
- The players take turns drawing the top card.

- Each player reads his card and decides whether what is says is true or false.
- If the card belongs on the player's board he places it on one of the spaces. If it does not, he puts it at the bottom of the pile.
- The player who fills his board first wins.

## Completing sentences

**To make**
- On strips of card write sentences with one word missing.
- Cut slots for the missing words (It is easier to do this with a craft knife than with scissors.)
- Make picture cards to fit in the slots.
You can also make this game by sticking self-adhesive fabric in the spaces and on the back of the picture cards.

**To play**
Children read the sentences and fit the picture cards into the spaces.

Slot for picture card.

The dogs chased the

on the ☐ bus

The ducks are in the

hit the ball

Sticky fabric squares

# READING ALOUD TOGETHER

Encourage your child to read aloud with you.

Choose books that really capture your child's interest.

The best way to bridge the gap between reading to a child and getting the child himself to read is to encourage him to read aloud with you. This helps to build the child's confidence and establish a fluent pace and rhythm in reading, which in turn helps him to understand the sense and the story, rather than just struggling to get the words right. Without the support of a fluent reader's voice a child often reads so slowly at first, because he is concentrating on getting each word right, that he takes in none of the meaning.

It is very important that children perceive books as a source of pleasure and entertainment. If they are to do this you must choose books that will engage their interest, emotions and imagination and which will encourage them always to look for meaning in what they read. Giving children reading material that is dull, repetitive or nonsensical makes learning to read very difficult indeed.

A child's early experiences of learning to read are crucial. He must find them enjoyable and rewarding. Although it can be a very natural and straightforward process it is very easy to put children off. On the next few pages you will find some advice on things to do and to avoid doing in order to make helping your child learn to read a pleasurable experience for you both.

## When to start

There is no way that it is possible to test children to see if they are ready to read. Even within the same family different children often start at very different times. The differences can be up to about two years.

You need to take your cue from your child. If you are used to looking at books together and reading stories to your child you may find the progression to reading together a very natural one. If you are not, you will probably find that you need to make a deliberate effort to do this before your child becomes interested in the idea of learning to read.

Here are some questions you could ask yourself to help you decide whether to try encouraging your child to join in with you when you read to him:

- Does he like books?

- Does he sometimes look at them by himself?

- Does he sometimes pretend he is reading?

- Does he show an interest when you point out words or write things down for him?

- Does he enjoy playing games with words and letters?

- Does he ask you what words say?

- Does he sometimes join in when you read stories he knows well?

- Can he retell a simple story in the right sequence?

# Choosing books for early reading

You do not need special "reading" books for learning to read. Choose books with a picture and one or two short, meaningful sentences on each page. The picture should show clearly what the words underneath say to give the child clues.

It is very important always to use books which have a strong story sequence. Even those with few words should have a beginning, a middle and an end.

Don't worry about the length of the words or the range of words used. Books which use a very restricted range of simple words are not necessarily easier to read.

You could use old favourites rather than selecting something new for reading together, provided that the books fit the above requirements.

Look at the contrasting examples below.

## Size of print

People often think that children's first reading books should have specially large print to make it easier to read the words. It is not the size of the print which matters so much as the space between the words. It is important that words can clearly be seen to be separate. Large print can be a disadvantage, especially if it means that not many words fit on a line so that the sentences become very disjointed.

my mommy
had a new
baby in the
hospital

my mommy had
a new baby
in the hospital

The squirrel is eating a nut.

The girl has red hair.

The words clearly match the action in the picture.

The words are accurate, but do not describe the action.

Tom ran down the road.

He fell over a dog.

He cut his hand.

The dog licked it.

In the above sequence the pictures give accurate clues to the words and there is a strong story-line.

Tom goes up the tree.

Up and up he goes.

Look at him.

Come here Tom.

Here there is no strong story sequence and the pictures and words are not well matched.

21

## First steps

*Where's the wolf going now?*

● When you have chosen a suitable book read it to your child and talk about the story and the pictures.

● When you read you don't need to point to individual words, but just run your finger slowly and continuously under the line of print.

*Do you know what that word says?*

● Pick out some of the key words in the story and show them to your child.

*Shall we read it together?*

● Suggest your child joins in when you read the story through again.

● Read the story through again fairly slowly, encouraging your child to join in with any bits she can remember. At first she may only be able to join in with a few words, but as she gets more familiar with the book she will be able to manage more.

*She swam towards the boat.*

*...towards the boat.*

● Adjust your speed to find the best balance between keeping the sense of the story and allowing your child to keep up. You will find that with practice you can gradually increase your speed.

● Give your child time to look at each picture to remind her of what the words say.

## Correcting mistakes

*The fireman used a house to put out the fire.*

*Wait a minute. I don't think that makes sense, does it?*

When you are reading with a child, or listening to him read, there is no need to insist that every word is read correctly. Children often make very sensible mistakes and replace words with words that have very similar meanings, such as "house" instead of "home". If a child makes a sensible mistake it means he is thinking about what he is reading, and not just saying the words he sees. Don't stop to correct it.

If a mistake does not make sense, stop and suggest he goes back to the beginning of the sentence. Read it with him to help him use the sense to correct his mistake.

## Prompting

If a child comes to a word he cannot read, suggest he leaves it out and reads to the end of the sentence. Then go back and read the whole sentence again and encourage him to guess what word fits into the gap. Give him a little time to find the right word, then, if he is still stuck, say it for him.

*The pony galloped towards the fence.*

*as fast as he could go.*

*The horse galloped towards the fence.*

In the early stages of learning to read it is not helpful to encourage children to sound out words. This is only helpful for fairly competent readers. However, knowing the beginning sound of a word can be a powerful clue to an unknown word.*

*Teaching sounds (phonics) is discussed more fully on page 42.*

## Progress towards independent reading

As your child's confidence increases let her voice lead the reading. Try dropping out and see if she can keep going. If she gets stuck join in again. Don't rush her to read alone if she is unwilling. Let her decide when she is ready.

For a while she may always choose to read things that she already knows off by heart. Don't worry about this. It is a normal stage in learning to read. Most people learn to read by recognizing on the page what they can already repeat to themselves.

Once she can read a particular book don't always expect her to want to read the whole story aloud. You could sometimes take turns to read alternate pages or read it yourself. Don't stop reading aloud to your child when you think she can read.

When you are listening to a child read, always give her your full attention. If you try to do other things at the same time she will soon form the idea that her reading is no longer important to you.

You will find that, as with other aspects of development, children take leaps forward in reading and then make no more progress for a while. Don't look for constant improvement. Give your child time to enjoy her new skills by reading lots of books at the same level and don't discourage her from going back to easy books.

## Things to remember

**DO:**

*Mmm... Good... Well done!*

- Build confidence at every opportunity. Learning to read is dependent on a child's belief that she can do it.

- Give plenty of praise.

- Be patient. Take things at the right pace for your child.

- Choose books that interest your child.

*Which one shall we have tonight?*

- Keep each session very short and stop as soon as your child seems to be getting bored.

- Encourage her to concentrate on the meaning of what she is reading and to make a sensible guess if she does not know a word.

*Can you guess what it might do?*

- Make sure each session is enjoyable for you both.
- Choose a time when you can be relaxed and give your undivided attention.

**DON'T:**

- Get anxious about your child's reading. It is more important that she becomes a keen reader, once she can read, than that she learns to read at a particular time.

- Expect rapid results or constant progress. Learning to read is often a very gradual process.

- Set specific goals for achievement.

- Think of yourself as teaching a child to read a particular book but as helping her towards the next stage in the reading process.

- Try to have a reading session when either you or your child is not in the mood.

- Criticize your child's reading or urge her to try harder.

- Make comparisons with other children's progress or encourage children to be competitive about reading.

- Spoil a story by making it a word recognition contest.

- Insist that every word is correct. Getting the meaning is far more important.

23

# SOME LETTER GAMES TO MAKE AND PLAY

Most of these games concentrate on helping children to spot the initial sound of a word and relate it to a letter.

At first when you play these games choose words that start with single consonant sounds, such as "bird" or "bat", not double consonant sounds, such as "bridge" or "black".

For a list of useful materials for making the games and some general points to bear in mind refer to page 16.

## Washing line

**To make**

Piece of string

● Cut out a long strip of thick card. (You could use a thin strip of wood.)

● Draw a line or stick a piece of string near the top of the card.

● Cut pictures of clothes out of catalogues or magazines and stick them along the washing line.

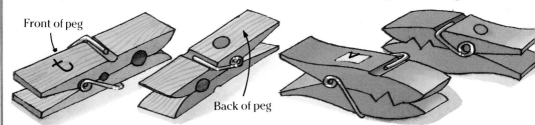

Front of peg

Back of peg

● Take some clothes pegs and on each one write the first letter of one of the items of clothing. You can write the letters straight on to wooden pegs. If you use plastic pegs, write the letters on sticky labels.

● On the other side of each peg put a small circle of colour. Use a different colour for each peg.

● Clip each peg on to its matching piece of clothing, as shown on the left, then turn the card over and make a coloured dot to match the dot on the back of each peg.

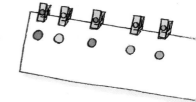

## To play

Take the pegs off and let your child enjoy matching the pegs to the clothes and then checking the coloured dots to see whether she has got it right.

Later you can vary this game by choosing words that start with a double consonant sound (such as "scarf") and writing the first two letters on the peg, or turn it into a word game by writing the whole word.

# Letter patience

## To make
- Make a baseboard about $10 \times 15$ in.
- Draw 15 equal spaces on it.
- Write a different letter in each space, except the one in the centre of the baseboard.
- Colour the space in the centre.
- Cut out a small card to fit each space.

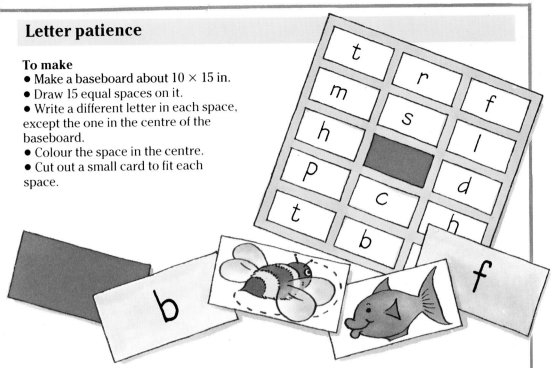

- Colour one card to match the space at the centre of the baseboard.

- On each of the remaining cards write a letter to match one of the letters on the baseboard.

- On the reverse side of each letter card draw or stick a picture of something that begins with the letter shown on the other side.

## To play
- Lay the cards at random over the spaces on the baseboard with the pictures facing upwards.
- The coloured card should be laid on the board but leave the coloured space at the centre of the baseboard uncovered.

- There will be one card left over. Hide this away without the player seeing it. The player starts by moving the coloured card on to the space at the centre of the baseboard. This will leave a letter uncovered.

- The player then has to find a picture of a word which starts with the uncovered letter. When she finds it she places it over the letter, with the picture facing downwards.

- She then has to find a picture to match the next letter she has uncovered, and so on, until she cannot find a picture, because it is the one that was hidden at the beginning of the game.

- The player counts how many moves she has managed to make and tries to beat this the next time she plays.

## Windows

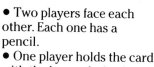

### To make
- Cut out a piece of card about 6 × 4 in.
- Punch six holes in it.
- Write a letter above each hole.
- Turn the card over and draw or stick a picture above each hole. The picture must show a word that starts with the same letter as the one shown above that hole on the reverse side.
- Find two pencils.

### To play
- Two players face each other. Each one has a pencil.
- One player holds the card with the letters facing him and says "Find me something that begins with . . .", naming one of the letters.

- The other player chooses a picture and puts her pencil through the hole underneath it. The first player will then be able to tell immediately whether she has chosen the right one.

## Word chain

### To make
You will need blank pieces of paper, about the size of postcards, a thick pen or crayon and some sticky tape.

### To play
- The first player looks round the room and writes down on one of the pieces of paper the name of something he can see.
- The next player looks at the last letter and tries to find something that begins with that letter. He writes the word down on a piece of paper and sticks it to the end of the previous piece.
- Continue until one player gets stuck.
- Count up the number of words in your chain and see if you can beat it with your next word chain.

You can play this casually over a day or several days and vary it by playing in different rooms. If you do not mind sticking things to your walls, it can be fun to stick the pieces of paper to the wall as you play. You can adapt the game to play on a journey by just saying the words instead of writing them down. To make it easier you can allow any objects and not just those you can see. To make it more difficult, restrict the choice to a particular group or category of words (e.g. animals, people's names).

# Three in a row

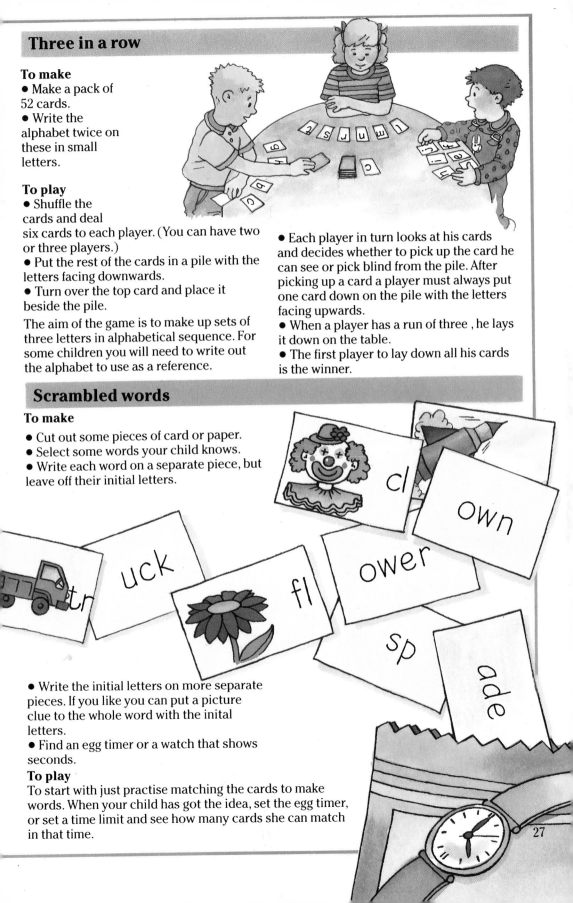

## To make
● Make a pack of
52 cards.
● Write the
alphabet twice on
these in small
letters.

## To play
● Shuffle the
cards and deal
six cards to each player. (You can have two
or three players.)
● Put the rest of the cards in a pile with the
letters facing downwards.
● Turn over the top card and place it
beside the pile.

The aim of the game is to make up sets of
three letters in alphabetical sequence. For
some children you will need to write out
the alphabet to use as a reference.

● Each player in turn looks at his cards
and decides whether to pick up the card he
can see or pick blind from the pile. After
picking up a card a player must always put
one card down on the pile with the letters
facing upwards.
● When a player has a run of three , he lays
it down on the table.
● The first player to lay down all his cards
is the winner.

# Scrambled words

## To make

● Cut out some pieces of card or paper.
● Select some words your child knows.
● Write each word on a separate piece, but
leave off their initial letters.

● Write the initial letters on more separate
pieces. If you like you can put a picture
clue to the whole word with the inital
letters.
● Find an egg timer or a watch that shows
seconds.

## To play
To start with just practise matching the cards to make
words. When your child has got the idea, set the egg timer,
or set a time limit and see how many cards she can match
in that time.

27

## Rhyming snap

**To make**

● Cut out some cards about 2½ × 2½ in. You can play with any number but you will probably want between 24 and 40.
● Make a list of pairs of words that rhyme (some examples are given below) and draw or stick pictures of them on to the cards.

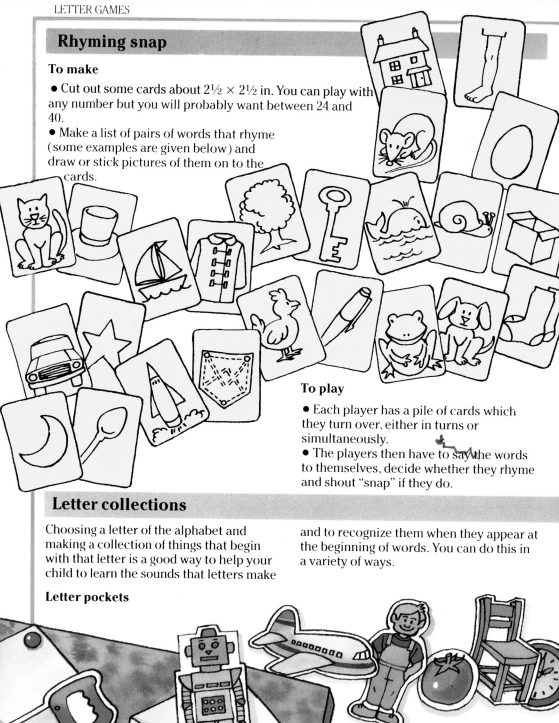

**To play**

● Each player has a pile of cards which they turn over, either in turns or simultaneously.
● The players then have to say the words to themselves, decide whether they rhyme and shout "snap" if they do.

## Letter collections

Choosing a letter of the alphabet and making a collection of things that begin with that letter is a good way to help your child to learn the sounds that letters make and to recognize them when they appear at the beginning of words. You can do this in a variety of ways.

**Letter pockets**

Stick envelopes to a big board or box. Write a different letter on each envelope. Collect pictures of things which start with those letters. Have fun mixing them up and then sorting them back into their envelopes.

## Pack my bag

### To make

- Cut out some strips of card.
- Write sentences on them similar to the ones shown below.
- Put them into a box or bag.

I am going to the beach. In my bag I will take a ball, a bucket, a boat and a...

> I am going to France.

> I am going to the moon.

### To play

- Take turns to pull out a card.
- When you pull out a card, you have to name as many things as you can that start with the same letter as the place you are going to.

## Tracing letters

### To play

One player "writes" a letter on another player's back. The second player has to guess what the first player has written.

This game, though simple, is quite difficult for most small children. They will need to concentrate quite hard. As they get better at it you can gradually progress to tracing three letters which spell a word.

### Letter table

Rr

Choose a low table, windowsill or shelf. Select a letter and together start collecting objects that start with that letter. You can spread this activity over several days. When you have exhausted the possibilities with one letter, clear the table and start again with another.

### Letter scrapbook

Buy or make a scrapbook. (A photograph album with self-adhesive peel-back pages is ideal for this purpose.) Write or stick a capital letter and its small letter at the top of a page and collect pictures or photographs to go on that page. Concentrate on one letter at a time but don't necessarily do them in alphabetical order. You could make a simple photograph alphabet book for a baby brother or sister by taking just one photo for each letter of the alphabet.

### Letter collage

Make a collage of words beginning with a particular letter. Make several and build them up into a frieze.

# ENCOURAGING READERS TO READ

Once children can read to themselves they still need continued support and encouragement if they are to develop into keen readers.

Many parents complain that although their children can read, they don't unless forced to. There are so many attractive alternatives that it is not always easy to get children enthusiastic about books.

As a parent you can help to create the time for children to read free from other distractions; you can introduce them to books they might enjoy and help them to develop their own tastes. Tempt and guide them into reading, but try not to nag or let books become an issue between you.

## Reading aloud

Do continue to read to your child even though he is now capable of reading to himself. It is the surest way to motivate him into reading to himself.

Read on a regular basis at times that suit you both and stop well before your child starts to lose interest. Allow time to discuss the stories you read and talk about the author and the illustrations as well as the stories themselves. For children who find it difficult just to sit still and listen to a story, provide paper and crayons so they can keep their hands busy while they listen.

## Silent reading

As soon as they are able to, children much prefer to read to themselves. Don't insist that your child continues to read aloud to you.

Help to create time for reading by developing routine reading times, possibly when you yourself also read silently. In any event, do let your child see you reading to yourself purely for pleasure sometimes. If you never choose to read, you can hardly complain when your child chooses not to.

Limit distractions such as television watching so that they do not consume all available time for reading. Read some of your child's books to yourself so you can still share and discuss them with her.

## Choosing books for children

Once your child can read you can still play an important part in her choice of books. Try to find things that will appeal to her particular interests. Making children laugh is a good way to get them involved in something, so look for books that appeal to your child's sense of humour.

Consider carefully the length of the book and the proportion of words to pictures to help you decide whether the level is appropriate. You don't have to stick to one particular level, however. Don't discourage the reading of easy books or old favourites and occasionally try out something that will challenge her understanding.

You may find yourself a little overwhelmed by the sheer volume of choice available in children's books. Many children's booksellers and librarians can give good advice and see this as part of their jobs. You might find it helpful to join a children's book club which will give you a limited selection to choose from at your leisure on a regular basis. You may find a particular reviewer in a newspaper or magazine gives good advice. There are magazines solely devoted to children's books and a number of guides to children's books which are published annually.

## Helping children choose books

Help your child to develop her own tastes by providing her with as wide a choice as possible and don't be critical of the choices she makes.

If you are worried because your child seems to have an insatiable appetite for a particular theme or for books that seem to have little to commend them, don't try to stop her reading them. Remember that she is at least establishing a reading habit and that we all enjoy undemanding reading sometimes. Wait until her interest seems

to be waning and then try to tempt her with something different.

Help your child learn how to assess a book by looking at the cover, reading the cover notes and notes about the author, and by flipping through and dipping in.

## Helping children use books

As well as encouraging children to read stories, it is very valuable to encourage them to use information and reference books. They need to understand how to locate the information they want – how to use contents pages and indexes, and how encyclopedias and dictionaries work.

One of the best ways of developing these skills is to pursue some interest together. Remember, though, that a child's interest in a particular subject usually needs to be aroused first, before he starts using books to find out more about it. Your own interest also needs to be real if it is to be a genuinely joint activity.

## Library visits

Establish the habit of making regular visits to your local library. Choosing from a wide range of books, without the pressure of buying, gives children more freedom to experiment and therefore to become more discriminating.

Ask the librarian to explain how to use the catalogue system, so that together you can find books by a particular author or on a particular topic.

## Other reading material

Magazines and newspapers can also feed a child's appetite for reading. Help him to find his way around a newspaper or magazine you get regularly so that he can find the bits that interest him.

Don't actively discourage the reading of comics, but do look at what your child chooses to make sure you don't find the contents offensive.

There are some very good books written in comic strip form. If comics are the only thing your child will read, try introducing her to some of these.

# WRITING AND READING

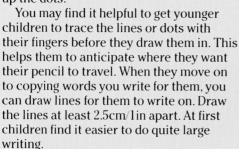

Writing is a way of telling another person something.

Encourage toddlers to use crayons and pencils.

There is a very strong connection between learning to read and learning to write. Being able to write a word will clearly help a child to read that word. In a more general sense, writing down things they want to say and then reading them to someone, helps children to appreciate that writing is for telling another person something.

Given the opportunity, most children start to enjoy scribbling with crayons and pencils while still toddlers. They often want to "read" to you what they have "written". This shows that they are already beginning to grasp the idea that squiggles on a page can tell you something and that there is a relationship between talking and writing.

By the age of four, most children are capable of writing some letters, usually those that appear in their own name. At five, most children are ready to start copying words. As their pencil control increases, their writing will gradually improve. Do remember that neatness in handwriting has nothing to do with intelligence and that too much insistence on it may constrain what a child has to say. It is important however, to develop legible handwriting. If, after two or three years of practice, your child's handwriting remains very poor, discuss this with her teacher.

## Tracing and copying

When children first start to write letters it is often helpful to give them letters to trace. Try using a yellow crayon (not wax) or highlighter pen and getting them to write over it in a darker colour. You could also do dotted letters for them and get them to join up the dots.

You may find it helpful to get younger children to trace the lines or dots with their fingers before they draw them in. This helps them to anticipate where they want their pencil to travel. When they move on to copying words you write for them, you can draw lines for them to write on. Draw the lines at least 2.5cm/1in apart. At first children find it easier to do quite large writing.

## Starting points and arrows

It is important for children to learn the correct way to form each letter of the alphabet as soon as they start to write. Left to their own devices, they often start a letter in the wrong place and move in the wrong direction. A wrong movement once learned can be hard to change and this can cause great difficulty when they go on to cursive writing.

Until they become quite confident, you can use a dot to indicate where each letter should be started and an arrow to show in which direction the pencil should move. For guidance on dots and arrows see the sample script on the opposite page.

# Styles of writing

There are a number of slightly different styles of writing for teaching to children. Opinion differs as to which is the best one to use. Different schools use different styles, so when you know which school your child will go to, it is worth finding out which style of writing is used there. The one shown below is the most common.

Only the small letters of the alphabet are shown here because capital letters do not vary in style. When children are learning to write it is best to concentrate on the small letters. Do remember this. Parents often make the mistake of teaching their preschool children to write only in capitals. You should, however, use capitals where these would normally occur, such as at the beginning of names or place names.

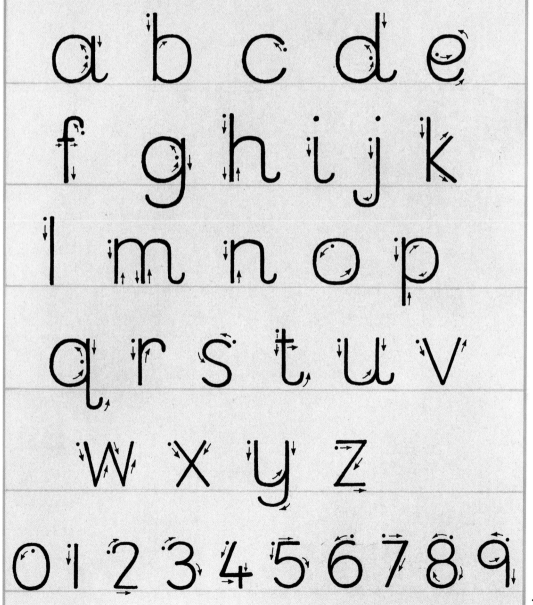

## Left-handed children

About ten percent of children are left-handed. Of this group some are ambidextrous, that is, they can use both hands. In the past all children, even those who were strongly left-handed, were trained to use their right hand for writing. In some cases this is thought to have caused stammering. It is now understood that children should be allowed to choose which hand is best for them. If, however, they can use both, it is sensible to choose one dominant hand and stick to it, otherwise they can get confused.

Writing with the left hand is not easy because it entails a pushing movement – right-handed people use a pulling movement. A right-handed person's hand moves along the page leaving visible what has just been written. A left-handed person's writing hand tends to cover up the letters which have just been written. Two simple solutions help to overcome this problem:

1. Get the child to hold his pencil a little further from the end than you would for a right-handed child.

2. Position the writing paper at an angle of 45° to the child's body.

Special three-sided pencil grips can be bought very cheaply. These make the pen or pencil fatter and easier to grip and can help a left-handed child to write more quickly and with less effort.

In the early stages of reading, children often like to point to the words in the book. A left-handed child is better off using a strip of card to place under the words and sentences.

## Mirror writing

Many children start by writing some letters and numbers backwards, especially b, d, 2, 3, and 7, or even produce superb mirror writng. Six and seven-year-olds often continue to do this. It is something that nearly always puts itself right in time, but do always point out the mistake and suggest correcting it.

## Holding pens and pencils

It does not matter whether your child uses pencils, crayons or felt pens to write with, but do check that, whatever she uses, she is holding it correctly. It is easy to develop bad writing habits by starting with the wrong grip.

They should be held lightly between the thumb and first finger about 1 in from the point.

## Pencil control

It takes a lot of practice to develop sufficient pencil control to write legible letters. Activities such as drawing, tracing, colouring, using chalks or paints, and copying or making up patterns can all contribute significantly to this process.

# SPELLING AND READING

People often think that a child who reads well should automatically be able to spell well. Good readers who are not good at spelling are often accused of being lazy. This is not the case. Spelling is very different from reading, and it is worth remembering that neither spelling nor reading are good indicators of general intelligence.

It is now known that writing a word down is a much more helpful way of learning to spell it than reading it, spelling it out loud or trying to remember spelling rules.

## Writing and spelling

If your child asks you how to spell a word, always write it down for her to copy or trace over. Don't take the easy way out and just say the letters. The movement of her hand will help her brain to recall the pattern of the letters.

To make this activity more fun, try using a highlighter pen which your child can trace over in pencil.

If your child finds some words particularly difficult, or has a list of words to learn to spell, get her to follow this routine:

LOOK at the word.
COVER it up.
WRITE it down.
CHECK it.

Encourage your child to write. Get her into the habit of writing messages, lists and letters. Find as many interesting and purposeful ways for her to write as you can.

mom
dont forget
swimming
tommorrow,
Tim.

Dear gran
I can ride
my bike.
love from
Nicky.

Saturday 20th
Today we
saw a film
about a dragon
It was very
exciting.

## Breaking words into sections

Encourage children to break words up into clusters of letters or syllables, instead of seeing them as an unbroken series of letters. This helps them to think about and remember how to spell them.

Help your child to practise counting the syllables in words and spot frequently recurring groups of letters.

1 2 3
in ter est

1 2 3
drag-on-fly

swim

## Using a dictionary

Provide a good, clear dictionary for your child and help her learn how to use it.

## Rules

Learning spelling rules used to be a popular way of teaching spelling, but they are no longer thought to be very helpful. They can prove helpful, however, for some older children (11-16) with severe spelling problems.

"i" before "e", except after "c", except for … ?

## Invented spellings

Do not expect too much too soon. It takes children time to learn to spell. They usually go through an invented spelling stage. This is important as it allows a child to explore written language without being too restricted by the number of words he can spell. Don't correct every word but encourage him to be careful with the words he uses most often.

# GAMES TO HELP WITH SPELLING

Any games or activities that encourage children to look carefully at words will help with their spelling. The more looking they do, the more they will start to realize when a word looks wrong.

Remember with spelling it is the look of the word and not the sound that is important. When finding groups of similar words for a game it is, for instance, acceptable to use "home", "some" and "women".

## Words within words

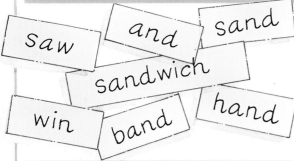

Write a word down for your child and see how many other words she can find in it. For very young children you can make the game easier by writing the long word down on one piece of paper and the small words on separate pieces of paper. Put in some small words which do not belong and get her to sort them out.

## Quick spell

See how many names of objects in the room your child can write down within a given time. Use a kitchen timer.

Give children time to check their lists carefully and make any corrections before giving them to you to check. They can often tell just by looking closely whether they have got something wrong.

Use a dictionary to help them correct any mistakes.

## Kim's game

Select a few words and write them on pieces of paper. Lay them out on the table. Let your child look at them for a minute or two and then turn the words over. See if she can remember the words and write them down. If she finds this difficult to do, encourage her to trace the words on the table with her finger while she looks at them.

## Letter patterns

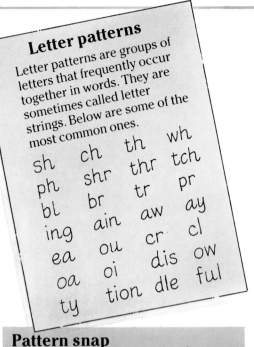

Letter patterns are groups of letters that frequently occur together in words. They are sometimes called letter strings. Below are some of the most common ones.

sh ch th wh
ph shr thr tch
bl br tr pr
ing ain aw ay
ea ou cr cl
oa oi dis ow
ty tion dle ful

## Pattern spotting

Take a page of a comic, magazine or newspaper. Choose a letter pattern from one of the headlines and see how many words your child can find on the page that contain the same pattern.

## Pattern snap

Make a game of snap in which children have to spot and match common letter patterns.

● Choose six different letter patterns.
● For each letter pattern find four words in which it appears.
● Cut out 24 pieces of card or paper and write one of the words on each card.
● Play as you would play normal snap.

brush
ship
push
washer

balloon
bull
really
ball

## Pattern pairs

You can also use the snap cards to play a pairs or memory game.

● Put all the cards face down.
● Take turns to turn over any two cards. If they contain the same pattern, you keep them and try again.
● The aim of the game is to collect as many pairs as possible.

best
listen
toast
step
maid
pair
air
stairs

● For very young children you can make the game easier by writing the letter patterns in a different colour from the rest of the word.

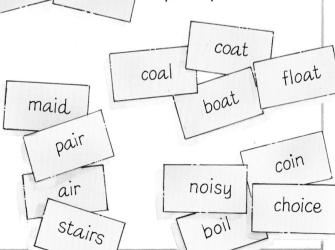

coat
coal
float
boat
coin
noisy
choice
boil

## Plasticine letters

● Roll out some thin strips of plasticine or playdough and use them to make words.
● Blindfold your child and get him to try and guess by touch what word you have just made.

## Down and up

```
m _ _ _ _ _ e
o _ _ _ _ _ s
u _ _ _ _ _ u
s _ _ _ _ _ o
e _ _ _ _ _ m
```

● Choose a word and write it downwards and upwards, as shown above.
● Ask your child to find words to go across, using the first and last letters already there.
● Show her how to use a dictionary to help.

## What am I writing?

● Think of a fairly long word which your child knows and uses.
● Start writing the word as shown.
● See how quickly he can guess what it is.

```
t
te
tel
tele
telev
televi
televis
televisi
televisio
television
```

This activity helps a child learn to predict what comes next, which is very important in reading.

## Silly sentences

train
talkative
rabbits
always
ignore
newts

chimney
children
have
itchy
magic
noses
every
year

● Write a word along the top of a piece of paper.
● Then you both have to try and make up a sentence, using, in order, words that start with the letters of the word along the top of the page. The sillier the sentence, the more fun you will have.

## Cut-out letters and words

● Cut letters or words out of the headlines in newspapers and magazines and use them to make up messages or greetings cards.

Good Luck in your swimming test

Congrat-ulations on getting married!

## Staircase

● Draw a staircase on a piece of paper.
● See how quickly the stairs can be filled in with words of the right length.

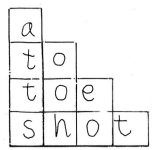

You can get children to use a comic or newspaper to help them.

Add more stairs to make it more difficult.

## Another staircase

tree
g
g
star
o
a
duck
i
n
g etc.

Staircases like this one are also fun to make. Three and four letter ones are easy. Five letter ones are quite hard.

## Spot the odd one

**To make**
● Find six counters or small coins for each player and a dice.

● On pieces of paper or card make for each player a chart similar to the ones shown below.

The idea is to make children look carefully at words that appear quite similar.

**To play**
● Each player in turn throws the dice and then looks along the appropriate row to find the odd word out.
● He covers the odd one out with a counter.
● If he gets it wrong he does not get another chance to correct it until he throws that number again.
● If he throws a number he has had before he misses a turn.
● The first person to place six counters correctly is the winner.

39

# READING AND SCHOOL

There is a wide variation in the way schools teach children to read, but it is now generally recognized by teachers that different methods* suit different children at different times, and that they have to vary their approach according to individual needs. Gone are the days when every child took turns to read from the same book.

Whatever methods are used, it is the teacher's own enthusiasm for books which is always the most important factor in successful teaching.

## Starting school

There are wide differences in the age at which children are ready to read, according to individual development, inclination and experience. Teachers in reception classes are trained to cope with this.

There should be no question of a child who can already read having to kill time waiting for the others to learn, nor of a slower starter having to struggle to "catch up", although many parents worry about this.

Each book in a reading scheme usually has a number or a letter to show its place in the scheme.

## Reading schemes

A reading scheme is a series of graded books specially designed for children who are learning to read. About ninety per cent of schools in the United States use some form of reading scheme.

Reading schemes can build children's confidence by taking them through a series of carefully graded steps. They and their parents and teachers have some measure of how they are progressing.

One criticism of reading schemes is that they concentrate too much on repeating words to the detriment of the story. Modern reading schemes, however, do tend to be much livelier and more interesting than those most adults remember from their own school days.

Because the books are numbered, critics also feel that they make some children unnecessarily competitive about reading and give others a sense of failure.

Some schools do not use a scheme and allow children to select freely from a variety of books. Schools often label the books that do not belong to a scheme with coloured stickers to give the teacher and the children an indication of the reading level.

Children should not be hurried through a reading scheme but need time to enjoy several books at the same level.

*See pages 42 and 43 for more about methods of teaching reading.

# Moves to involve parents in the teaching of reading

Until fairly recently most teachers held firmly to the view that teaching children to read was entirely their responsibility and that parents should not interfere. This narrow, completely unsubstantiated view is fast disappearing and the majority of primary schools now actively encourage parents to work with them.

The level of involvement expected from parents varies from school to school. Many send home reading books, usually with a notebook or card suggesting to parents what activity they should do that evening. This might be hearing a child read, reading to them, reading the book out loud together or discussing particular things in the book. They might be asked to play a reading game or go through a list of individual words.

Some schools have bookshops or a special "library time" when parents and children together can choose books to read. Some invite parents into the classroom to read with groups of children.

Some schools issue booklets or hold meetings explaining their approach to reading and the ways in which they would like parents to help.

It is important that you feel clear about what the school is doing and what they expect you to do. Most teachers, though busy, will be quite happy to explain things to you.

If the school does not involve you, just continue reading to and with your child, choosing books that you both enjoy.

## Working with the school

It is always sensible to try to work with the school as far as possible. If you feel happy about what is going on, you will not find this difficult. Don't, however, be tempted to push your child, thinking that this will please her teacher – if a teacher asks you to read five pages, don't read fifteen.

If you are unhappy with the school's approach to reading try not to let your child become aware of it. It is difficult for young children to cope with differences of opinion between home and school. But do tell the teacher if your child finds the books sent home for reading are boring.

## Reading tests

Some schools assess reading progress by giving children tests. The tests are devised by educational experts and tried out on a large number of children before they are sold to schools.

Results are given in terms of "reading age". It is not easy to simplify procedures, but, in general, if there are twenty questions in a test and in the trials most of the ten-year-old children get eighteen of the questions right, then all children who score eighteen will be said to have a reading age of ten.

Modern tests do show whether children understand what they are reading as well as whether they can recognize words. The exercises in the tests are often sentences with a word missing. The reader has to choose from a group of words to complete the sentence, for example,

**The bucket was full of (sky, water, elephant).**

Reading tests given annually can help teachers to check each child's progress and to identify which children need more individual tuition. Most teachers would not test a child under seven. None of the reading tests is considered reliable for very young children.

Some individual tests can help to pin point particular problems. These are called diagnostic tests.

Critics of reading tests feel that they encourage unhealthy competition both between children and between schools.

# METHODS OF TEACHING READING

There has always been debate about which is the best way to teach reading and over the years all sorts of different methods have been devised to try to make learning easier.

Today, teachers tend to rely on the four main methods described here.

There is no conclusive evidence that any one method is superior to the others. Most teachers tend to combine a number of different methods to form their own particular approach. Different children benefit from different methods at different stages.

## Phonics

This method relies on children being taught the alphabet first, learning the names of the letters and the sounds they make. Once they have learned the letter sounds they begin to blend certain ones together to make simple words.

r-a-t  c-a-t  s-a-t  m-a-t

In order to give children reading practice in these skills the story books have to be rather contrived, so that all the words are regular and can be sounded out. It is extremely difficult to write books with phonically regular words that are interesting for children to read.

Ned set the wet
hen in the bed.

There are other disadvantages to using a phonic method as a first approach to reading. Learning isolated sounds is very abstract for little children. It means nothing to them and they usually find it boring. They also have to concentrate so hard on sounding out words that they are unable to think about the meaning. It is possible to say words correctly without having any idea what they mean. Children taught exclusively by this method will learn and pronounce nonsense words quite correctly, whereas if the words were in sentences they would know immediately that they had no meaning.

For these reasons the phonic method is not usually taught until children have a good grasp of the basics of reading. Older children, however, who are finding reading very difficult, often discover a phonic approach works well for them.

## Look and say

In this method children learn to recognize whole words or sentences rather than individual sounds. They look at the words, they hear them said, and then they repeat them.

Twenty years ago it was common practice to use flashcards (individual words written in large letters on cards) in teaching by this method. The cards were held up for the children to recognize, but because there were no clues to help them, most of the time children just made wild guesses.

It is now generally recognized that it is better to show a whole sentence first, preferably with a picture;

Sarah is reading a book.

| Sarah | is | reading | a | book. |

then a set of matching word cards to put under the sentence; and finally just the word cards to make into a sentence.

In this way children can get meaning from print from the earliest stages of learning to read.

# Language experience approach

Mommy took our dog

The dog was naughty and ran away

We went to the park

Pages join together to form a book.

In this approach the teacher uses the child's own words to help him learn to read. The words may be a caption for a picture or a little story made into a book.

At first the child tells the teacher what to write. After a while the children can copy over the teacher's writing and can eventually write their own words down.

Many teachers use this method as a first approach to reading. Reading their own words helps children understand that the written word is for communicating meaning from one person to another.

## Context support method

When children are learning to read it is very important that they use books that really interest them. They cannot manage too many new words in a book, though, and it is difficult to write interesting stories with a very limited number of words.

Yes, he was sure of it. The scarecrow was slowly waving his arm.

The scarecrow waved at the driver.

To get round this problem some books are being produced which give two versions of a story. A long version is often given on one page and on the facing page a shorter one.

Sometimes the longer version is at the bottom of the page and the shorter version in speech bubbles. The child hears the long version before reading the shorter version himself. The more limited vocabulary of the shorter version is brought to life because the child can relate it to what he has already heard.

This is a relatively new way of teaching early reading. It does help to make the printed word more interesting and meaningful for a child. If you come across books with a long and a short text, it is well worth trying them out.

## Some other terms

Here are some other terms you may have heard mentioned:

**Big books**. These are used by some schools to enable a small group of children to enjoy reading together, or to look at the pictures while the teacher reads.

**Decoding**. This means "sounding out" the component parts of a word.

**Paired reading**. This term is used to describe the activity of an adult and child reading aloud together. At times when the child feels able to read on her own she nudges the adult, or taps the table, to signal to the adult to stop reading. As soon as the child starts to struggle, the adult joins in again.

**Sight vocabulary**. All the words a child can read right away just by looking at them.

**Word attack skills**. This term covers the strategies you present to children to help them tackle new words – looking at pictures, reading on to the end of the sentence and coming back to a difficult word, or sounding out.

43

# READING DIFFICULTIES

Talk to your child's teacher about your worries.

The age and rate at which individual children learn to read varies widely, as with most other aspects of development. Most children learn to read somewhere between the ages of three and eight. For some the process of becoming a reader can take two or three years; for others everything seems to click into place extremely rapidly and within six months of starting they are avid independent readers.

However, a small percentage of children do encounter particular difficulties in learning to read. There are a number of possible causes.

## When to worry

Because of the wide variation in the age and rate at which children learn to read it is often hard for parents to know when to be concerned by a child's apparent lack of progress.

The best general advice is not to start worrying until your child is seven. If no progress has been made by this age, you need to take some action. It is not sensible to think that if you ignore the problem it will go away. The older children get the more difficult it becomes to deal with their reading problems.

Read together for a few minutes every day.

## What to do

Read through the checklist on the opposite page to make sure you are giving your child the right sort of support and encouragement and that you do not have unrealistic expectations of your child.

If you are still worried, tell your child's teacher and make an appointment to see the headteacher to discuss the situation with her. If there appears to be a severe reading problem she may suggest, or you can request, an assessment by an educational psychologist.

Provide plenty of opportunities for your child to write.

## Special teaching

Children who are finding reading very difficult can often be helped in school by a specialist teacher.

These teachers usually teach a small group, or even just one child, at a time. Care is taken to use books which have a high interest level but an easy text. With this kind of extra help most children can overcome their reading difficulties.

Sometimes older children, parents and other adults are recruited to come in and give extra help to slow readers, under the supervision of a specialist teacher.

## Parents'checklist

If your child appears to be finding it difficult to learn to read, ask yourself whether you are giving her enough of the right kind of help. Read through the list below to help you to decide.

• Do you give your child regular help with reading at home? Five minutes a day is much better than half an hour once a week.

• Do you give your child plenty of time to look at a book before asking her to attempt to read it to you?

• Are you using books of the right level for your child? You need easy books to encourage fluency and understanding of the story, but not something babyish which will undermine self respect. A book that is too hard and makes reading slow and uneven is impossible to understand.

• Do you provide plenty of opportunities for your child to write? Remember that writing helps both reading and spelling, but there needs to be a purpose to writing.

• Does your child understand that you have confidence in his ability to read? Try not to communicate to him any worries you have about his lack of progress. Never let him feel that you expect him to fail.

• Have you talked to your child's teacher? She may herself be concerned about your child's progress and be able to suggest further ways in which you can help at home, or she may feel that you are expecting too much and that your child is progressing to the best of her ability.

• Do you still read to your child regularly ? Enjoying books together will give her the motivation to learn to read.

• Have you had your child's hearing and sight checked by a doctor? Problems with either of these will clearly affect her ability to learn.

## Dyslexia

Some children who experience difficulty with learning to read may well be performing normally in all other subjects. (In time, though, the inability to read will inevitably hinder nearly all school work.) These children are often diagnosed as dyslexic, although not all children with reading problems can be accurately assessed in this way.

Dyslexic children frequently spell in a very bizarre way and generally have problems with any task that requires sequencing. They know which letters to write but they put them down in the wrong order.

It is a hard struggle for dyslexic children to learn to read and spell, and this is often made worse by people who do not understand the condition, believing them to be lazy or stupid.

In the past ten years, however, there has been a great deal of research done in this area, so more is now known about how to help dyslexics. They need very special teaching, with a highly-structured programme used daily. Those who have a mild form of dyslexia often respond very rapidly to this treatment. Those who have severe dyslexia need a great deal of time and patience. They nearly all do learn, though they may always read slowly and need a good dictionary to help them.

There are several associations which provide useful publications on dyslexia. These are listed on page 47.

# THE INSTANT WORD LIST

The Instant Word list is a list of the 300 most important words for reading and writing in the English language. It was researched by Professor Edward Fry from Rutgers State University of New Jersey, who discovered that these 300 words comprise nearly two thirds of all written material (books, newspapers, letters etc.).

This list can be used for instruction or as a test for your children. Words on their own seldom have meaning for a child, but if you use them in a sentence (i.e. in context) they are more likely to be read correctly.

## First hundred

| First 25<br>Group 1a | Second 25<br>Group 1b | Third 25<br>Group 1c | Fourth 25<br>Group 1d |
|---|---|---|---|
| the | or | will | number |
| of | one | up | no |
| and | had | other | way |
| a | by | about | could |
| to | word | out | people |
| in | but | many | my |
| is | not | then | than |
| you | what | them | first |
| that | all | these | water |
| it | were | so | been |
| he | we | some | call |
| was | when | her | who |
| for | your | would | oil |
| on | can | make | now |
| are | said | like | find |
| as | there | him | long |
| with | use | into | down |
| his | an | time | day |
| they | each | has | did |
| I | which | look | get |
| at | she | two | come |
| be | do | more | made |
| this | how | write | may |
| have | their | go | part |
| from | if | see | over |

## Second hundred

| First 25<br>Group 2a | Second 25<br>Group 2b | Third 25<br>Group 2c | Fourth 25<br>Group 2d |
|---|---|---|---|
| new | great | put | kind |
| sound | where | end | hand |
| take | help | does | picture |
| only | through | another | again |
| little | much | well | change |
| work | before | large | off |
| know | line | must | play |
| place | right | big | spell |
| year | too | even | air |
| live | mean | such | away |
| me | old | because | animal |
| back | any | turn | house |
| give | same | here | point |
| most | tell | why | page |
| very | boy | ask | letter |
| after | follow | went | mother |
| thing | came | men | answer |
| our | want | read | found |
| just | show | need | study |
| name | also | land | still |
| good | around | different | learn |
| sentence | form | home | should |
| man | three | us | America |
| think | small | move | world |
| say | set | try | high |

# Third hundred

| First 25<br>Group 3a | Second 25<br>Group 3b | Third 25<br>Group 3c | Fourth 25<br>Group 3d |
|---|---|---|---|
| every | left | until | idea |
| near | don't | children | enough |
| add | few | side | eat |
| food | while | feet | face |
| between | along | car | watch |
| own | might | mile | far |
| below | close | night | Indian |
| country | something | walk | real |
| plant | seem | white | almost |
| last | next | sea | let |
| school | hard | began | above |
| father | open | grow | girl |
| keep | example | took | sometimes |
| tree | begin | river | mountain |
| never | life | four | cut |
| start | always | carry | young |
| city | those | state | talk |
| earth | both | once | soon |
| eye | paper | book | list |
| light | together | hear | song |
| thought | got | stop | leave |
| head | group | without | family |
| under | often | second | body |
| story | run | late | music |
| saw | important | miss | color |

---

# OTHER USEFUL INFORMATION

## Book clubs

Book club sell books at discount prices, usually in return for a promise that you will buy a certain number of books a year. Several times a year they send you information about the books on offer and you order them by post.

It can be a great advantage to choose books at leisure, in your own home, and most children enjoy belonging to a club and receiving packages through the post.

**Beginning Readers Program**, Grolier Enterprises, Sherman Turnpike, Danbury, CT, USA 06816

**Children's Choice**, Macmillan, 6 Commercial, Hicksville, NY, USA 11801

**Disney's Wonderful World of Reading**, Grolier Enterprises, Sherman Turnpike, Danbury, CT, USA 06816

**Early Start**, Macmillan, 6 Commercial, Hicksville, NY, USA 11801

The following book clubs run a number of different children's book clubs which operate through playgroups and schools:

**Scholastic Book Services**, 730 Broadway, New York, NY, USA 10003

**Buddy Book Club**, 4343 Equity Drive, P.O. Box 16628, Columbus, OH, USA 43216

## Book Parties

**EDC Publishing**, 10302 E55th Place, Tulsa, OK, USA 74146

## Dyslexia

The following organisation offers information, help and support for dyslexic children, their parents and teachers:

**The Orton Dyslexia Society**, 724 York Road, Baltimore, MD, USA 21204

# INDEX

First published in 1988 by Usborne Publishing Ltd, 20, Garrick Street, London WC2 9BJ, England.
Copyright © Usborne Publishing Ltd 1988.                  American edition 1989.
The name Usborne and the device ☳ are Trade Marks of Usborne Publishing Ltd.